We Are the Fire

BY TOBY OLSON

Novels

The Life of Jesus
Seaview

Poetry

Maps
Worms into Nails
The Brand
Pig/s book
Vectors
Fishing
The Wrestlers & Other Poems
Changing Appearances: Poems 1965–1970
Home
Doctor Miriam
Aesthetics
The Florence Poems
Birdsongs
We Are the Fire

Toby Olson
We Are the Fire

A Selection of Poems

A NEW DIRECTIONS BOOK

ACKNOWLEDGMENTS

Of the poems in this volume, the following have been published in limited editions: "Fishing" appeared as a Perishable Press book; "Cotton Wood" and "Priorities" were in the Perishable Press book *Doctor Miriam;* "Sparrow," "Yellow Bird," "Night-Light," "A Very Hot Day," "Rocks," and "Turns" are from the Perishable Press book *Birdsongs;* "Standard-5" and "Standard-11" appeared as *Two Standards* from the Salient Seedling Press; "Brother Moon" and "Just This" were in the Landlocked Press book *Still/Quiet;* "Sitting in Gusevik" was a Black Mesa book; "The Florence Poems" were published by The Permanent Press; "The Spot" and "Smoke" are taken from the Membrane Press book *Home;* "Standard-4" appeared as a broadside from Aviator Press; "The Trumpet Vine" was a Salient Seedling Press broadside.

"Tools," "Incest," and "The Father" were in *The Wrestlers & Other Poems,* published by Barlenmir House. "Incest" and "The Father" also appeared in the author's New Directions novel, *The Life of Jesus.*

Some of the poems here appeared in the following magazines and anthologies, to which grateful acknowledgment is made: *Anima, Boundary-2. Conjunctions, Cottonwood Review, Delirium, Goat's Head, Handbook, Intrepid, The John O'Hara Review, Montemora, New Directions in Prose and Poetry, New Letters, #, Occurrence, The Painted Bride Quarterly, Poetry Now, Sumac: An Active Anthology, Sun, Sun & Moon, Tamarisk, Tracks, Tractor.*

Manufactured in the United States of America
First published clothbound and as New Directions Paperbook 580 in 1984
Published simultaneously in Canada by George J. McLeod, Ltd., Toronto

Library of Congress Cataloging in Publication Data
Olson, Toby.
    We are the fire.
    (A New Directions Book)
    I. Title.
PS3565.L84W4 1984   811'.54   84-4772
ISBN 0-8112-0913-X
ISBN 0-8112-0914-8 (New Directions paperbook : pbk.)

New Directions Books are published for James Laughlin
by New Directions Publishing Corporation,
80 Eighth Avenue, New York 10011

Contents

Author's Note

The following poems, together with *Home* and *Aesthetics* (Membrane Press, 1976 & 1978), stand as better than half of what I wish to save from the years 1970–84. "The Florence Poems," a series occasioned by the death of a dear friend, is offered here intact. From "Standards," a series I see no immediate end to, I've included six. The word "Standard" refers to old popular songs, and each of the poems was begun by taking the lyrics of these songs quite seriously, trusting in their significance to whole generations of people. Remnants of the lyrics, both intact and transformed, can be found in all the poems. The stories of the songs are the stories of the poems. We are the fire that lights the details.

Toby Olson

For Miriam

The Trumpet Vine

This plant that rises
    pushing itself snake like
against the house
is honeysuckle,

   & it reaches up
to find some purchase
    on the shingles & tucks
its small & delicate
toy trumpet flowers in there—

it smells good
but is just as easily identified
by sight.

On the other hand
I never saw the trumpet vine
    (easier by far to recognize
when it's in bloom)
that grew along your porch
& covered a good portion of its roof
when I was young.

I never lived in your house
but I spent a good deal of time
coming & going.

Away from there to here
where I can see
    beyond their constant names
even the change in
delicacies of weeds in my yard
& the new bucklings
in the trees from winter winds,

I have to wonder
how I spent those years
    passing the unseen trumpet vine,

my head usually down
& elsewhere.

Always
it seems better in the past;
it's very hard to live
where body is
      & I get startled when I think
I didn't know you well at all
& that some details of this yard
         will inevitably escape me
leaving only
partial understandings.

On the other hand
      the trumpet vine
tho once cut back by accident
is curling still
         while we're away
sending its clear flowers out;

they may well bloom for someone else
who may also
be missing them.

I mean to say
I could have danced
with horns behind my ears;
      we could have danced together
snaking the vines on our arms.

At least I wore your bathrobe once
& made you laugh;
      the doctor told you
no intercourse for two weeks
when you were 82,
& we both laughed.

At least
I have your blood in my vines—
I mean my veins . . .

2

Theme Music

When they play theme music from *The Godfather*
I am genuinely moved.

The movies are amazing.

The way at the wedding at the Galaxy
we drift together
in tux and white dress on the dance floor—

well, I am born free &
Is this the little girl I married?

On the screen, in the movies, the people
drift in and out of relationships
of places: Miami-
        Sicily-Havana.
some are pulled backward through open drapes
onto balconies, to the sound of music. they
double up and bow.

At the Galaxy, they play
theme music from *The Way We Were*
        memories/light the corners of my mind,
dancing
with you in my tux I am born free
into the movies.

But *The Way We Were*
is not the way we were
ever,
        and in the movies
people die and return again,
a pair screw standing up against closed doors
at the wedding,
        a man wakes up sleeping
with a horse's head.

And here, at the Galaxy
a hush falls
    over the darkened room.

To the beginning strains of theme music
from *The Godfather*

the bride and groom,
whose moves are anticipations of tragedy
    (but in a movie,

dance awkwardly
into their song.

Standard–4, These Foolish Things (Residual)

Each time I see a crowd of people
    (evidence of a lost chance of mastery)
standing at a stoplight at Flatbush Avenue—
possibly
it is raining—
reminds me of you.

    & the ghost of you sings

we
winged it in the nature of Country & Western
dark bars in Corpus, you
    sweet bucktoothed Mexican girl
    hugged in the arc of parking lights
    lit up the beach and the Gulf of Mexico
foolishly.

An airline ticket to romantic places?
Chicago,
braces of high-school sweetheart
    cutting the lips
        not the time or place
inappropriate.

What goes on daily
the impropriety of staring
        flint of heartland straight into
the dead center of the heart, is
flesh memory,
cleaved in twain.

Each time I see a crowd of people
the light changes
        the ghost of you sings
inappropriate,
                    out the classroom window

maybe you'll be there:
hair tied back in a pony tail
walking the bright side of the avenue

going away
from this talk of a Black African
growing-up story:

   "He held
   Njoroge's private parts
   with a pair of pincers . . . "

you/ in a variety of gowns and faces

-these fragments
-these foolish things

I want something.

Standard–5, I Can't Get Started (The Fan)

I need a little coffee
but I'll take a little satisfaction instead.
Bright morning, a clear head
seems appropriate
    but I'm a little messed up rising
    from a troubled sleep, cough up
a few mechanical tears in the cutting wind
going out to write this.
I could use a little flushing of the system
to get started.

  last night
  we walked the streets of P-Town much longer
  than I'd thought possible
  given my oyster legs & sore arms.
  she paced me
  carefully, into the shops
  and I stuck with her
      hardly able to even have eyes
  for the passing women
  I was so tired. we thought
  we'd go see *Female Trouble* at 10
  but she could see my slump
      we decided against it & came home
  & read a little & got to bed late
  I must have dreamed
  but I don't remember.
      My head's a little clearer now.

The Eastern-
King-Bird sits on the bayberry stalk before me;
he's clear of eye. The pleasure
    of his body is like a bird-book
picture, the demarcation
of wing color and beaked head. He fled

from the feeder which was too close to me.
He sits looking at me
        from a little under a safe distance
were I a cat. Does he know this?
Of course he does:
probably the size distinction. Turns his head,
feathers slide and meld on his neck
like a rich feathered fan.
        How do you think the forms
of fans were invented, anyway?
The Royal Fan—The King Bird.

Seaward— where
there is nothing but fog cover
a few miles out
under
a day moon, Factory Boats
& the local fishermen dropping their nets
        that fan out catching
whatever is left,
where it is clear (no
Sea of Remembrance)
while the cat hunts here
& the birds too.

Would
that we could
old friend, have lived
something akin
to these
        half casual motions
quiet, lighter
than we were
(hunters also)
turned in
to relationships:

wing fan passing over the bird's sharp eye
for a moment; the cat makes her move,
bird lifts

and settles in again as she passes,
occasional eye shade of the fan
    I need a little satisfaction
    but I can't get started.

I remember the picture of a woman sitting
on a sheet-draped couch,
    your wife naked and posing, holding
a fan maybe (stripes
of Venetian light) and then
that Western bar painting you made from that:
white sheets turned to satin
or blue silk against
her whiteness, her new fullness, hair
a little longer
    than her hair
(in starlight) that
modest guarding
of fan discarded, turning
discomfort in the snapshot
to ease.

    what was it you wanted to give me?

a little intimacy? a twist
of relationship?
some satisfaction?
or female trouble?

charted—

Fans flash under the sea catching
the light
    off fish;
there are two birds now, the third
a cat; that
revolution of species
did not succeed
tho, she is flushed out.

As if oiled,
the body in the painting
on velvet, in surety; I remember
more, old friend
        your delicate art,
the challenge of a little
photographic realism
& romantic handling,
her real passing
along the couch I awoke on
sweating in starlight.

what we needed was satisfaction,
a little eucalyptus in bath oil:
to be object of another's care regardless
of neurotic motive,
love, or the fact
that her head was elsewhere. she'd
bring us tea,
the blanket and the soft chair,
as if our sickness were physical, and
such care healed.

Now it is raining. there's
nothing in it for rejuvenation.
        it'll soon clear.
the King Birds puff in the wind and rain,
but the sea's clouded.
there's female trouble stirring
in the closest bush.
gestalt of wing fan breaks
in the passing storm.
        the coffee is cold, half drunk
and unsatisfied.
fans fold their memories
and the patterns burn.

started.

We thought to know her better
than we knew ourselves. we did not
    know ourselves, each other
the ones we lived with
(live with)—

      I see her often
not in the painting, in photo
but moon of her ass
    in starlight; in a way
we lived together
in weather: the each
and quiet possibilities of change
within continuity.

down at the bay
the quay is full of fishermen
and their catch: blues & striped bass,
the passing women in white shorts bending over
the rows of fish,
           the lovely
silken slime of death on their silver bodies
and on the backs of the women's thighs
oil, mixed with sweat.

A Moral Proposition

She took me to her house and explained
her husband
   was in some way defective
& would I not consider?

I was 19 and ready
to leave next morning for California
which she knew) she was a nurse.
outside
   it was early evening, no trees
   yet in the project,
ground broken in places for new houses
for flower beds.

I thought Jesus! this is *not* for me, but she
cajoled me —English
they had just arrived here
childless— very starched
and nunlike in her nurse's dress
& efficient.

Early evening, lights were low, we sat
on the couch together
proper, talked in a soft voice
analytic. and like a mother.

And I was very close
to being convinced, could see
the bedroom thru the door. why not
leave a child here?
Jesus! this is for me, I thought

potency, I thought
this is the perfect gift,
transcendent; she was a nurse
   I was her patient

12

—she turned to me
a little flushed,

and when I saw her lust
I left.

Priorities

"You have to take things as they come"
is a worn currency;
    depending upon your mood:
an answer to fear of age
or alcohol.

2 o'clock
is maybe the worst part of the day:
    means you got thru half of it
but still have a way to go.

Today
before you left for work
you came to me where I was working,
looking for scotch tape,
    and then you lifted and turned your dress
and fixed the hem with it.

                    temporary
desire raging
even in morning's look above your knee:
I take it as it comes
and almost as important—
such simple ingenuity.

I had a wife, once
would tape her spit curls to her cheeks:
    she had a troubled need
to have her hair done
carefully.

That makeshift hem will hold for a little while,
and that's enough.
I do not want to make too much of this.

It's only that the day began with lust
and some discovery,
and that your hem's sufficient.

On the Road to Perry's Farm

Almost naked riding on a bicycle she comes
along the road from Perry's farm.
The basket
over which her breasts bob, carries
some fresh corn
from Perry's. Her bikini
tight on her brown body, willfully
she shifts
        the 10 speed to go
up the hill.
Will
she stall, fall
        and scrape her body, will the corn
spill its yellow grain and silk across the road?

Almost naked
she makes it up the hill.
I enter Perry's farm and smell
dogs & fish.

Standard–7, An Austere Song for Sal Mineo

So easy is the myth of Public Figures
that certain transparency
in which we are amazed to find them.

No sooner does the mind
turn to expansive showplace of vision
in which the child-star is encumbered
but that he grows.

Perry Mason
the fatherly trial-lawyer is effeminate
        raises orchids & gestures
his limp hand
tracing subtle figures in the air

& what truly is age
or masculinity, but a fixity
a way of placement.

Somehow
the breeze today is structured
austere & arch: it moves against the windows
like architecture.
this is a good day for mythology.

In the movies
a distant sound of thunder, a freight train
a music:
        each action is imbedded
with music,
guide-light of the myth.

But today is also
a place of private actions of people,
streets of dreams & houses

over which
birds sing their music
& disjunction
in the quality of this air
which does not enter our lives
necessarily, tho we wish it.

Sallie—
I am thinking of a song, some theme music
& a context in which a Public Figure
in my own life is moving
        a young psychotic & rebel
& the song is wordless, the melody
hardly perceptible, but that doesn't matter.

That most poems, too, stand in their way
as fiction, doesn't matter
either.

The face of the past president fails.
It is a sad reminder,
his mother
his good father, & the way
each one falls out of placement
confuses our histories—
that matters.

But I am thinking of the movies, almost
hearing music. you were always
surrounded by songs, rebellious
& moody,
            as if your heart was
more serious
than our hearts, who were
locked in a similar age:

the 50s, those songs
so inextricable from memory, I can almost
hear them
        still as they form

what a heart is,
that false
communality of the past.

But this is no day for weeping & discovery.
It is a day shot thru with sunlight
all morning
        & by afternoon
the people
are half free from covering
half joyful, even tho
they might be going to funerals,
have troubles:

        they live with song.
This is incredible light.

And I am thinking of the movies, almost
hearing that music. you were always
good for a joke:

Gene Krupa, your sweetly ridiculous
age there. jokes
about casting you as Moses
        in roles of great subtlety
your name used always
derisively, in friendly conversation.

The myth you lived in
was aegis
under which children
of your own age
found what?
                but a placement
& contrast, a charming music:

we were all
adolescent-child-stars
burning in myth—
but that was not you.

Sal,
today's air has a quality like crystal.
You can see right thru it, as if
thru the film's transparency
the music & thunder

    as if it were not mythology
& the newspapers reached & joined you
into character of Brooklyn Street-Youth
now heart stabbed in California.

what a sad
& useless posture we come to
in want of articulate life.

move over) Let the light air
bird songs, thunder & the music
come down from its invisible structure

to mourn you, Dino:
that was a faker of memory, as if
life were art
regardless of the quality of either.
this was not your life
tho it was ours.

He who lives as a Public Figure is not living
life there. Sal,
I imagine you could have seen with me
into the strange indifference
of today's sky.

It is architectonic & beautiful
like the history of Public Figures

but it is only
a quality of air.

The Spot

Who makes of his wife a goddess, is subject
to certain depression
    thinks he's a king
or trash unworthy

to possess her even
live in the same house
with her.

    either way her faults
pierce his groin like needles
also he walks around with a sick head.

Who loves her and then
seeks other women
faultless & perfect smelling
and longs for the nectar, he *is* trash
or a false king on his property.

He who loves her truly
however, will kiss a rash on her body
take in the smell of her breath in the morning—

    seeing her face in the textures of concrete walls
    in the bellies of other women
He discovers his real value
and finds his spot.

Brother Moon

I ignore you Brother Moon so long
before I know
you're back again

It's night)
and in the living room she stood
enchanted—
                    or at least
she got up for you
at 3 AM.

            At 9 she tells me
how you shone for her.
I was asleep,

and now her gown's opaque.

Sitting in Gusevik

I was sitting in my cousin's house, at the start
        of a loss of ten pounds (the fjord
    a block away)
in the middle of the longest day
in Norway.

some fires would burn on the hills at midnight
(still light) and they'd be setting rafts
of logs ablaze,
tho in avoidance of trout farms,
adrift, across from the steel factory
at Gusevik.

Gusevik, which I
had just found out was my real name
but in this case was a house,
                                outpost
    in which a man and his wife now lived
who had changed his name
when his father'd bought the place
from my cousin, Oskar's father: Ommond Gusevik,
around 1910.
                        I was sitting there
outside it was
well (you know) Norway, back
in a time when sex was dirty and air was clean
        where I could see across
my cousin's potato farm
across the road
and a white horse walking slowly
in her fields
close to its time of foal.

We were sitting in my cousin Oskar's house
downstairs, in the coffee shop. his daughter

Johanna, who ran the place, was cooking
carbonnade
              and a drunk came in
who loved her
obviously, had come in
to be close to her, and I
        was still getting used to the fact
my name was no longer Olson
but Gusevik.

the drunk
was trying hard, but he
could get no tumble.

                        Johanna
would laugh a little
and scowl and raise her eyebrows
in our direction

                    and the drunk
obviously thought
to play to us a bit
and said in perfect English:
"Business is business, but love is bullshit."

Sitting here now in America (NYC)
in this room,
and out this window
snow-capped terrace railings & the slush
already running in the tiles' grate.

birds
that come this height
are truculent and peck
        at anything that's in sight

blue jays & few
sparrows, stalwart pigeons come to sit
on the refined steel of the water tower.

the cat squats
in danger upon
    the dark ledge, her body
    darker still against
white snow;
crazily
close to death but giving in
to a business sense
she sees the way I watch her
watch the birds;

I see
the old hotel
across from me, the cluttered
minuets
of men and women
    doing business, and the birds
and cat that stand apart from that
and me.

I hit
the ashtray's edge
put down the cup
and think:
        "it's dark here today."

        It's darker still in Norway,
where
in summer we had rowed
across the fjord
    were almost caught in a sudden Norwegian rain
and sat on the porch of the house in which
my great grandfather was born,

Tobias
upon whose porch I sat
6 years old with a cup of Swedish coffee
in Illinois.

                    memory
like his son and grandson stops
prematurely and like their deaths.

the house is gone, the other
across water,
faces a factory.

Well,
the drunk was saying
        what he thought we'd like to hear.
he had a leer.
his talk was American Ingenuity,
                    but he
could not manage well
and we
were a little uncomfortable. Johanna
finished her cooking up and got rid of him.

We talked
    and left the house at midnight
light of sun still visible
        presence on town street

& drove to the public bonfire
to a vacant lot where it was fading,
    people gathered
around huge ember logs and sang
religious songs.

I hung to the window post, and then
was fading west
to L.A.

to Lois
who woke me up with tea. it was
the heavy porcelain navy cup
she'd put on the bedstand,

and I
was brought from dream by entrance
into the dream of tea smell.

I was doing business there
with white woman (or) white horse, in haze
of flared nostril smoke,
                    so that
the dream was led by intention
into the presence of Lois,
        (face / in tea haze)
and this
outline
of dream wife
        was sweet horse breath, but then
was tea until
I was awake,
                and Lois
blowing the steaming tea across
my sleeping face

& I was asleep & awake.

Personal history is a dream like that
and like the Indian speaks of what it can't remember
but knows is true, and says
in extenuation of where it started from,
its history: "It is said."

It is said—
the old folks carried
100-pound sacks of grain
in the 19th century
up the steep escarpment behind the house
to the other, older houses
above the fjord
        (were very tough
And Oskar said that

when the Nazis came, the food supply got short
and you could see the poor tobacco
the people were forced to grow
flame like tiny torches
in pipes across the fjord.

Today
Norwegian wood
floats in a cove across
from Gusevik beside
        the steel factory in which
Johanna controls the food concessions and the drunk
works, and I
blessed by American Ingenuity
row hard against
the tide from the North Sea
in the face of that,
i.e.:
The Log Cabin
a Restaurant on a Farm
a Name Change.

Lois,
it was a dream as if
the jasmine in the tea were a simple tool,
        tho magical, that could
unlock some history

as if
the woman in the dream (the horse), her breath
were the real thing, and I
had changed somehow
to a rarity
of feeling where
the tea's technology was a sacredness
in that I was consumed by a history that was
a part of me, was gene-like

and my life,
        for lack of a better word, was tribal
so that business was
a part of love & cluster
like the valley of Kvinesdal

in which I rowed
        where everyone was my relative
and write about, as if
there could be answer here

in America (NYC) sitting in Gusevik, my skin
but in this room
where lives are only private
& so is love and business.

They were kin,
    were very friendly
we went to the cemetery.
my cousin's husband took me to a soccer game.
we ate good food.
        they certainly seemed to love my wife.
even the doors of their language
opened a bit. the virtue I made of ignorance
of their speech, to nod and smile
and gesture when I could not understand, gave fruit.
Johanna sent me the valley's history book
I could not read.

the scale says I have lost 10 pounds, have changed.
I who had no business within that place.
I of the changed name.

Incest

A young boy decides
he wants to go to bed with his mother,
who has given him
ample indication
that it's all right to do that.

And because the boy's mother
and father sleep in separate rooms, there's
no problem about the boy's going in
which he does one night
but in the morning they can't get separated.

It seems
the mother's vagina
has for some reason begun to expand
and started to pull the boy back inside her,
which creates a problem
because he is 10 years old.

But thank god he isn't a big boy
and the mother is able
to strap him to her body
with two of her husband's belts, tho
most of him is still outside of her
but if he hunches up in a ball
she can cover him with an old maternity dress.

Now the father is quite shocked
when he notices but the mother is very coy
and delicate and says she's been to the doctor that day
and that she's been pregnant for months.
She tells him their son
left just that morning for camp.

Now the marvelous thing
is that the father becomes very attentive again
to the mother after 10 years of ignoring her,
and begins to bring flowers and candy.
And the mother feels delicate and feminine
again, and the boy keeps moving inside her.

And then after 4 months (
of being fed in the bathroom
of close quiet talks with his mother
of hearing the tenderness between his parents)
even his head goes inside
and the father finally
goes away on a business trip and the mother
goes to an out-of-the-way hospital.

When the father comes back the mother
tells him about the miscarriage
but neither of them are too sad
and take great pleasure
in having their son home from camp.

From that day on
the father sleeps in the mother's bedroom,
the son takes
the bedroom his father has vacated
and begins to get interested in girls.

The Father

This is a very
traditional
            story about a father
who is cut from tin, and a son
who has surely only
created this image of his father

The mother
plays a very small part in this:
she helps
            the son carry
his father to bed at night;
she reminds the father to
go thru
            motions of eating at dinner time

The father is truly
cut out of tin, and though he has hinges
at his knees and hips
from the waist up
he is very rigid
and his arms are only hinged at the shoulders

The night before
the father takes the son out on weekends
the son creeps into the bedroom
where his father sleeps
and paints
            an appropriate smile
or grin, on the flat surface of the father's face

Now the son imagines
there is a real father
about, that he sleeps under the bed of the tin
father, and that he is rounded
like the son is

But the son can't
                    look under there
afraid, that what he imagines
might be true. The mother
plays a very small part in this
tho she tells him always
to sleep in the center of the bed

One day
the father takes the son out in the country
and as long as he stands
with his flat body
cutting the wind
everything goes along fine

But while they are walking
out of a wood and over a rise in a meadow
the son trips
and the father turns to help
him, and is caught by the wind

Now imagine how
the father reaches out to the son
as he is lifted
                    slightly off the ground
he
picks up speed and is waving his legs
and stiff arms
to keep his balance. Think of the son
dumb-struck and helpless
running after
his father who misses the first trees
but is struck
by a hanging limb
and is ripped in half
                    at the abdomen:
the one sound the son hears—
the tearing of a piece of tin

Now the mother
plays a very small part in this
and when the son gets home, she says:
where is your father?

"I suppose he's hiding under the bed
again" And the mother says
well, be sure to sleep right in the center
of the bed tonight

and before the son goes to sleep
he begins to feel
his skeleton, eating his flesh away
from the inside.

The Florence Poems

For Morris

1—Grave Side

I come here not
to bring you back
    tho it be heart-felt
& pathetic,
the insane wish:

two sisters
sitting on a blanket, alone
on the beach in the sun—
gone.

It is also selfish, all
so that a world's particulars
in which I was standing
every day every day
remain (mine),

& against that killing
talk of community
as if we were not always
alone.

The uphill light
biting at the permanent stones
is capricious too.

I am thinking of our secret names.

2–A Domestic Song

He who brings home the bacon is often
lost in the fire that smoked it

He himself is the fire
& cannot pull his eyes back far enough to see it

He lifts a glass to her
who is a coat rack for his riches

She waits the days out
under the smoke clouds of their arrangement.

But the man who is the bacon
doesn't dance or sing her praises

And whatever god it was that snatched her
is cursed with conviction

She was no coat rack
this was no arrangement

All his riches
become dross in proof of her value

He can only be the other man
in passing.

3—At Ryder

The two women
on the beach
in the sun
        are waiting for someone,
or else resting
after activity: a few shells,
some dusty miller
& two nice stones on the blanket
            which curls a bit at its edges
in just a very light breeze.

But I make assumptions falsely
about postures —younger
than my mother, older than my wife—
        they are not between things,
they wait for nothing,
are not resting,
if
they are in anything
it's 3 children playing in the sand,
the 6 gulls riding
        on the cold swells
beyond them.

The white woman & the black man
stroll calf deep in the surf,
        parents of these variously shaded children;
the man is coal black,
his wife's a little pink at the edges;
staying
between the children & the deeper water,
they splash a little
& play there.

And down the sandy path from the parking lot
a tall young woman in a large red hat

maneuvers a wheelchair
     containing a thin old man
in a blue swimming suit
& comes to the water's edge;

she locks the wheels;
he rises a little
     on thin arms & slips
awkwardly into the surf
         where he is turned gently
& starts a slow & graceful sidestroke out
to where the gulls sit.

At the edge of these current events
the two women
     begin to prepare for leaving.
A strong breeze rises up
& all the blankets along the beach
begin to wave.

4—Another Domestic Song

Nothing becomes so difficult
that we can't live with it,

even the way you shift
& turn your carcinoma in the night
with resignation.

The last thing a man wants to do
is the last thing he does—
& other glib words.

Because it was so difficult
he left the room again:
        no place to rest his eyes
not even outside
not even closing them.

Because it is so difficult
he entered your room again

—nothing but glib words.

5–The Allergies

The cat sits in the sun
on the desk
            cleaning herself,
her pupils gathered;
in the place
she sits the hair she gracefully
kicks up.
            settles around her
      in the sun's
shadows.

In the sun
all energy she has becomes
the innate mechanism:
her long tongue
& her years of sitting
in other places
always in the sun.

I sit again in this room
waiting for voices that don't arrive.
      There is a certain
fragility I've come
to expect in the lives of other people
& now my own;
I've put a thistle feeder
close by
            in the open air,
probably the wrong place:
no birds—
you get what you pay for.

      Listening for other voices:
that twig in the bathroom window
hitting & scraping against the glass—
what else to remind me of

but change
& its attendants: death, & the very edge
of spring's coming
buds, & then green leaves.

If outwardly
the sea right now
        seems misted over,
it's these cat hairs
hanging a kind of woven garment
in the air
between some vision & the bay.

About thirty yards away
some orioles flit
in the skeletal bush
I couldn't see yesterday morning;
        fogged in & raining,
I stayed in most of the day
adjusting the pots under the leaks.

But the orioles strike out together
gaudy in flight
        (their orange armor) quaking
the dead bush as they leave it
in parody of life,
& the cat turns her head in her preening
& we both watch it—
putting it off.

To think of the structure
of the roof only
        when the rain comes in:
I mean
here in the sun,
like the body's barriers,
shingles wear in the grooves
insidiously, in that we do not see it

or do see it
       & put things off—
put what off?

Smoke curls from the cigarette in my hand;
the cat's hairs curl in the smoke & sun:
       you would have been nervous by now,
your fear of cats,
that innate mechanism,
your vision to the bay cut off.

The backs of my hands
are a little like shingles: a field called
lichen planus,
the cause of which isn't known:

I touched
my grandmother's back
in her cancer bed
& then my hands turned red.

I think I am now in a field, called
Anaphylaxis.

Like a planet
(Jupiter, the astronomer says)
burns away in its dark location in the sky,
you had to die
a little distantly & alone,
       & the rest of us
cooked in our allergies
in this foreign place.

       It's brought home every day, that
fundamental thing
we have put off;
now under this high thunder cover
I itch for reclamation of such
waste.

Like in
plants growing on a shocked plane,
         heavy seeds blossoming in the pores,
the innate mechanism of growth,
the backs of my hands
shine sometimes;

imagine
a man standing
with palms over his face;
in that privacy,
in fog,
he'd be a red warning beacon,
putting you off.

No one to talk with anymore
about certain things,
that little
history we had, of which
surely the larger history
is made:

         flavors of ice cream, flowers,
movies & politics,
the singular
cuttings that we made
into the woven textures,
opening the air
a bit at least
to a kind of sighted
human matrix.

I think now
of the flavor of Michael,
      about six summers ago,
turning red in the surf at Longnook—
his intended wife, the seemingly
bright coming of his life—

            now hung from a tree
three days ago, by his own hand
in accordance with some law
of medicine;

not Christ's priests,
philosophers,
nor psychiatrists can put it off,
        nor the spectacle of its effects,
that strange affinity among us:
growth of body & mind
gone wrong,
        & the small taste
on the backs of my hands—
Flo,
the little histories
& the large:
such the law.

I see
the boats out on the bay now
        turning in the sun;
the light
even at this distance
glinting off them.

Red sails in the sunset,
but it's morning:
        the sails are white,
the sea's blue-green,
yellowish clouds.

At horizon
a bank of fog, a hazy
demarcation, a soft line at which
the eyes unfocus
& the sea quits.

Are we better out of it?
Is there less pain there?
Why do we
put it off: what is the law?

It's 8:15; the sun
begins
        to give up; the sky darkens
even the dark thunder cover
pressing against it;
it starts to rain.

I place some pans in the house
for the rain that is falling
inside,
& the cat moves from the window
into artificial light;
        even in the rain
your finches have discovered the thistle.

Soon enough
I will have some songs to sing.

Flo,
I begin to think
only these carcinomas
don't put it off.

I've placed my hands into that field
& can join you now.

6–Tail

The kids across the road
are flying kites this morning
in the fog.

Usually
when the fog comes
it's very still,

but there is breeze enough this time
and they rise quickly and go
almost out of sight.

Standing
mostly in the same places
on the ground

the kids themselves
often disappear
and then return again;

somehow
the invisible kite strings don't tangle;
the kids aren't fighting.

For space,
for a little time
within that space, we continue—

about a mile away
some dogs are fighting
in space and time;

the kites continue
to appear
in the air.

This comes on the tail
of finishing
a poem for you;

you keep coming back like a song
I'll continue to sing
and keep you alive.

The places where you lived
& their information:
    you in the medicine cabinet,
in the Scotch broom along the house,
a spot of blood on the bed's undercarriage
insidiously left behind,
& the razors in your clothes.

Poor philosophers,
we long for a ceremony of some kind,
& then rain comes out:
    the gurgle of water in the leaders
whose name is also
Flo.

And the river rises in the rain:
specifically
    the Pamet River
running from Ballston to the Bay
& back again
        (in rain & tide)
a kind of ceremony
I'll make nothing of.

Inadequate philosophers—
It seems so strange:
you are a kind of
    constancy against change.

The rain gives you up
& an iron sun comes out
& with it wind—

you're there in the damp & golden brush
in hints of the little golden birds

in the brash air.

8–Getting Up Again

     I don't really pretend
        to understand it, Florence:
gin in our drinks,
sitting in your back yard among flowers,
          some cheese & crackers on the tray,
& the hundreds of little eyes
of the new blueberries
looking at us;

     we're laughing & talking—
about fishing,
about some of our nutty experiences
in the close past or distant;
we may well go to the movies later,
or stay here
& get a little drunk.

Some shriveled leaves
at the edge of the blueberry patch—
the cultivation marks
of the tent caterpillar—
get me to remember a young child dying
when I too was a child:

the story of blue paint under his nails
his mother had wept at seeing
as he lay in the coffin—
     some tangle of difficulties there
a few days before
when he was alive & mischievous—

how cut the pain from such ties,
give back life to the living?
. . . whenever she hears of crib-death,
& all the chipped paint in the world
reminds her.

But all the little dusted eyes of the blueberries—
almost at the edge of my tennis shoe,
          ready to be picked & eaten—
pull at my gin-pushed gluttonous appetite
& I can't stay with that past
& be appropriately sad right now.

It is also true
that the boy's mother is now around sixty,
has seen her other children grow up
& be happy.
She lives in Hawaii.
          Who can deny she weeps about him at times,
but who can begrudge her
the warm pleasures of that island?

This place seems like an island too sometimes
          (so close to the sea & bay);
it's hard to pass up
the colors of the changing surf
as the sun hits it,
& there are days when gulls
& the windy sand veils on the dunes
can take your mind away.

OK:
this talk of islands
turns me to thinking about the girls
taking their swimsuits off at the nude beach;
I've just enough lustfulness in me today
to attend to them,
          but the gin helps
flip my attention to the beach itself
& backward to other beaches,
in California, & a soft high school
oasis in Arizona.

I'd gone swimming with the one I loved that time;
it was very hot; the raft sat

in the middle of the lake,
  & we stroked out to it;
it was far enough,
& we were alone out there
under a dry sun.

I was just 14;
I loved her a lot,
  but had never touched her;
she lay with her soft arm against mine,
& that was almost enough for me.

After we'd cooked for a while,
I got on my elbow & looked down at her,
was moved by the onyx
& copper choker she wore:
  it was half dry in the sun;
it looked cool & hard
on her pink baby skin—

only in color
was it like the necklace of yours
that Miriam has—

OK, Hello,
here I am thinking of you again.

I drink my gin
in the presence of the flowers
you planted & tended,
then turn to the way Morris will tend
your grave
only about a mile away.

  I'm sad & teary for a moment or two;
then turn to the way
we talked about that mystery novel
with such pleasure;
then I begin

50

thinking of Miriam, & *her* jewelry
on *her* skin.

I suspect
some approximation of this
happens in the heads of all of us;
    I can see the way these blueberries turn
& ripen in the sun;
some of them are still blood raw—
immature, invulnerable
& tasteless—

it's the softer ones,
that are dusted robin's-egg blue,
I lust for—

    I'll keep trying to say goodby to you
so I can say hello again.

9–Whales

In the morning
when the air seemed ancient
in the room where lovers' lamps had burned,
he woke
to discover her absence in the bed:
at first light it was
his dramatic hand entering
that empty space.

And also
as in a cheap movie or novel
the rumpled sheets & stale air,
the moral in the transience
of the bright fire
of their short wicks;
        the perverted message
mildly attenuated in the particulars—
lamp, table & bed—
change coming in small doses
until it seems like constancy.

And so he might have been lonely,
might have risen & gone to the window
thinking he saw light there
or the evidence of it:
        illumined smoke fog of the morning,
not lamp's light
but the first hint of the sun.

The whale lay on the beach in low water.
It was the size of two houses
seen against the men's activities:
some carrying torches,
        yellowish fog lights in the mist,
illumined the ones cutting the melons out
& the vague sense of initials

52

carved in her head.
       They were all busy,
but it was the whale's
fruit & her presence
commanding them.

And he stood at the window
full of rage & loss—the emptiness
of his private bed behind him,
      the work of the poachers on his beach—
& searched the initials for the name of his adversary,
but it was too foggy:
the carving was only an emblem,
strange & figurative
cut in her head.

I see all this thru eyes
of the sad lover in the window,
      him who I have half-created;
tho he be hazy & unresolved,
he's therefore real,
like the people I live with daily
& know as well.

The literal source
is an old photograph of the beach
above Fisher
      (circa 1890)
in which at low tide the sand
is covered
with beached Pilot whales,
& a dozen or so men,
too well dressed for this place,
are walking among them
& seem startled,
as if shopping
in some new store.

Where does the head end,
& where does the body begin?

     They placed the benign mandibles of whales
upended, as arches of entrance
into the yards of boat captains—
marks of vocation,
& maybe reminders of fear & conquest—
who walked close to the jaws
of whales
many days, for business

(. . . as if whales grew under the ground
& died coming out
     fighting to leave it).

In Magritte's magic
animated movie
a fabulous whale steers to the shore
     where a man in a bowler (the poet of course)
waits.
The whale beaches herself;
she opens her mouth:
a flower grows on her tongue;
Magritte picks it,
& the whale
winks.

And I think it was night-hunter Spider
who came upon a sleeping whale on the Ivory Coast
& didn't know it—
           "Well,
     may be some treasure trove in this cave"
& he went in & the whale swallowed him
& it swam away.

And Spider saw the bones of the others digested
& he took the torch that he carried

& held it under the spine of the whale
    where the whale's life source was
& the whale
started to die & rock toward the shore
& it rocked Spider to sleep.

There's a movement against change in the Sea
& Spider slept for a long time & distance
& woke finally to the sound of activity:
    men outside
who were cutting the whale up for gain
& the knives coming in close to Spider
like in a magician's box.

And so he lit his torch
& held it under the whale's spine again
& the whale gave up
    a last yawn at the tickle—
& Spider burst out of the whale's wide mouth
like a warrior
& the men were startled
& thought him the dead whale's
avenging spirit & they all ran away;
    & Spider owned the fruit of the whale
that had eaten him.

A wind off the bay this morning
coming in lightly;
    low mare's tails in the sky
with tips up
promising good weather,
something of the shape of whale's spouts
though they lay horizontal—
from giant whales then
struggling
from the ground.

there
are a few boats out there;

it's calm enough for them:
fishing boats & a few with sails
move slowly
        against the horizon
in moderate breeze enough
to push them—
lightly
& yet seriously.

In the old days
before the vacuums of factory boats
        it was stars & fish that steered them:
navigations of head & body, the two poles
pulling them
even to the Georges Bank
for profit—
who came home
literally frozen sometimes
        & stood in snug-harbor,
a room cut in the fireplace
to thaw them.

John speaks
of the gone days of the Traps,
        those indiscriminate devices
that caught everything:
mostly mackerel for gain,
but fish to be wondered at,
        porpoise & dolphin,
even occasional
small whales.
John keeps listing the names of the dead:
the fishermen
along with the fish.

There remain six spheres of influence:
stars & moon
when visible to steer them;

then satellites;
        then hawks & gulls
of profounder interest;
the society of boats sitting on the sea,
and below these bodies
        the source of their living:
the silent culture
of fish.

It is taking me a long time
        to get to the point, Florence,
but the point is complex: has something to do
with the anatomy of a whale,
the issue—
where does the head end,
where does the body begin?

Below the sacred & scarred berm
the whale
        lies awash in the incoming tide
in the evening;
the scars
are the shards of her own body
where they have cut her up;
            what's sacred is beyond the wealth
& the property;
it's these leavings
that are not left—
        they go into the sea with the tide,
into the bellies of fish:
it's a very old story,
but it is hard to take.

Here in the reflections of our own death
is our triumph:
        55 years lived in the knowledge of it,
one & a half in its presence.
Having known it

& then felt it; having turned
to it
& gone on from that:
        the whale looming in our daily presence
dead on the beach.
In the last year & a half
we were with you:
        that was community—
cold solace for the heads of the living,
but this is where the body begins.

With a turn on the substitute log trick—
one in which the living appears dead—
Ninawa,
the Inland Whale, lay silent
in Fish Lake
        waiting for Toan (the bastard child)
to mistake her body for timber
& walk upon it—

difficult to imagine
a log that size,
but it is more difficult
to think of a whale come into our human
presence in this way—

        thus was the power transmitted
that blessed Toan,
that helped him to riches
& the head of the household at Pekwoi.
Ninawa brought him some understanding also,
& he could bury his mother, Nenem
when her time came
with considerable grace.

But the trick of Spider is different
(a man of various illusions,
        who can actually change himself .

into most anything: be born,
die, & be born again).

       It was a trick of light
& surprise
that sent the men running;
they had knowledge of the whale's death
in its stillness,
but they felt guilt in the salvage
(the head & the body):
                   thus
    when the Trickster Spider
came forth with his torch blazing,
their thoughts went quickly
to revenge magic;
because they'd felt death was an accusation
they were severely stunned
by a circumstance
in which the dead appeared to live again.

When the man turns back from the window
the light is changing
& the lamp at the bedside,
    now that the room's in half shadow
as sun rises,
is found to be burning
& lighting the bed up
where the gone lover had lain.

The shards of the indentations
of the lover's corpse
are still present,
   & he knows—
were the light lower,
the shadows a little more dramatic—
the log trick could apply:
      the head & the body of his lover
alive in the bed again.

But the last
remnants of fog burn away;
the room gets flooded with light,
& the obscuring
mercurial
shadows of drama are gone.

He gets back into the bed,
reaching to turn the useless light off;
he lies down in the place
where his absent lover had slept.
        He can feel the smooth shell of her face
over his own—
he sleeps like a log.

There's a slow closing of light on the bay;
some of the mare's tails
begin to tip,
        & over them
a few larger clouds come in.

But the sun has some fire left
though low in the sky,
        & though the breeze picks up a bit
some of the sails seem still & have
turned red.

The gulls under the satellites
turn slowly now,
under the hawks sitting on the air
above the sea.

The fishing boats with names of fish
on their hulls, still navigate over
where they think the fish are.

        Florence, do the graves
swell up? I know the grass upon them

grows toward the sea;
so do the heads of the coreopsis
followed by their leaning bodies;
so do we.

And I can see what's left of the whales
out on the beach
as the tide comes in;
      as the tide comes in
the flesh cut from their bodies
is lifted away;
the swells cover up
the places where the melons were cut;
they seem to be swimming
as they part the waves.

The initials start to become visible
as they seem to move:
      I can see the shards
of our secret names
cut in their skulls.

I imagine us sleeping
in their massive forms:

      Sperm—

Pilot—

Body & Head

*

You had a way of living
in the pleasures of this design
    we all seem to accept daily,
but there is none.
I think you were firm in knowing that.

You went on from it,
& had a way of living with each gesture
    & each event, so that a kind
of what I will call wholesomeness
lit it up.

You "lit it up"—
I like the sound of that—
a little like rockets
    blooming over the wharf in P-Town
this last 4th.

So much for the poverty of metaphor:
those brief & impotent sparks
in a dark sky.
    It is of course down here
under the rockets always
that we live
(lived).

The light that touches
the autumn olives in a breeze
can make their leaves glint in the night:
    it is the full moon, but it's
the undersides of the olive leaves
that have the silver.

That's better.
We all share in the power of the light;

at least we own
    a particularity of reflection,
if your secret name
is Luna.

But all this keeps us very lonely
& the moon,
consistent with this language, gets
eaten away,
    & it is only
the aura of its presence
that sustains us
till it comes again to thrill us
back to our privateness.

Flo,
I have tried hard to love you
as I love myself.

Now
into the perfect
community of our isolate lives
I commend you & your secret name,
dear Florence,
& I commend my own.

A Frame

Now it is raining
Its first few drops as always
    slanting against the window
one comes to learn about
just sitting, & then sun comes out
& right away goes in & it starts to rain again
left to right.

I never had a vision. I've had
a few dreams that seemed
possibly significant
    but I wouldn't bet on it
I think I like that.

Christ! these few
beautiful living objects, leaves
throwing the rain off, 4
relatively huge
    slender trunks of gingko,
squirrel touching his damp body against them,
his dew body)   It's early morning—

not the tales
but the details—
& now the sky darkens & the details
minus obscuring light
are clearer,

distant thunder.
It's going to storm
& the sockets behind me crackle.

My Moon Girl

I took a lady out
into the breath of her own desire,
the obvious melody
of an amusement park, when I was 15 years old.

She had more
craters in her face than I had that year;
she sat near me
in the back seat of the car,
but was hiding her face.

How have we learned to trust, love
be gentle, give out
more than we take back,
treat things other than economic?

She was a blind date, wanted only
a little blindness from me.
        I remember I loved
the ancient
moonscape of her face
she turned toward me
only in the dark tunnel of love;

I kissed
the umblemished
liver of her soft lips, but I wanted
to touch my moon girl's face.

The Clasp

You were my heart's desire, she said—
   that same game:
the past tense, divided
self & the public utterance.

   we were at the senior prom and her
necklace kept
falling down into little cleavage
enuf for me at 18) her mother, always
smiling and fixing the clasp.

But here (16 years later
it is her mother's face and not hers
draws me to lust.

We always thought you'd be a priest,
the girl says, or a doctor.
I dreamt about you last night.

   her mother grins over her shoulder,
fixing the clasp.

Smoke

I remember your body it was dancing timber
smell of eucalyptus burning
the endangered house

      and stood apart in the woods together
in smoke, and revealed your breast to me
I was 9 years old.

Each
experiment with love starts
with a body on fire at a distance
      a woman always
standing in full length across the room

Timber: the aureoles of your nipples
I could not touch

your skirt was moving in smoke
your ankles, covered with leaves.

Cylinders

My neighbor digs in the earth, the rich soil
he has brought together
    there in his garden against the wind.
Under his blue hat, white shirt, and hands
a glimpse of the hearty and large
green leaves, and a little red of the rhubarb
where he is tending
    and bending down to it,
fingers among the stalks.

It's early in June, a late spring,
a few flowers still on the honeysuckle,
first buds
    of portulaca
have not appeared, the weeds
have not gone seriously to seed yet,
        no indoor petals to float—
rose or day lily in bloom—
and we've neglected to buy petunias
for the planter.

We have
the green beginnings of rattlebox,
a little old-field-toad-flax,
a few juniper,
    strut of purple and gold finch,
and two large cement cylinders
(drainage devices) to be set in,
edge of the new road they've cut

    —cylinders for the rain
that won't sink into soil, but sit
glistening and ineffectual
on the new blacktop.

I watch
the hawk float in low over the scrub,
touches of pale yellow, gray and rust,
no more than six feet above it
and close enough. I'd say
      marsh hawk, hunter (harrier),
presage
of what skillful darkness?
It looks like a sunny day at ease, but
cylinders for the rain—
and now a few clouds come in.

    Donna was a little tipsy
    when she came over—
        Papa Joe could die soon.
    He says at the fish store
    "I've got cancer;
          I get the fish for nothing."

The drone of a dozer to my left.
I can only hear it,
but it shakes the house.
It's beyond the frame
I count on.
    Little shakes
to be honest, but ominous
of something—
sure the house'll hold;
it has through many winter winds I hear
in times I have not been here.

        Nor have I seen that river
I got out of you, Becky—
which river? in New York City?
But you met boys there,
and one suspects
    from sudden shyness and your smile
to kiss them, hold hands at least.
what? 16 years old?

You were happy then, but you
seemed always happy: *The Happy Immigrant*,
name for a musical or old movie.
I don't pretend to know
what happiness was about in your terms
exactly ("Mother"?)—
        grief beyond my experience
of grief, but very happy.

A quick wash on the window, the drops
distinct and accountable,
        to bring in, but obscure, light;
there's little of it:
a few clouds draining now,
the tentative
                coming of fog over the bay,
my delicate line of horizon
no longer attenuated, but it's a spring rain.

The cylinders begin to darken on the hill;
the drain holes in them catch light;
the cut of the new road, its primitive
sand, reddens.

    There was a light in Gracie's house
    all night; come to find out
    she died yesterday.
    Simply, we had not noticed it
    in daylight.

Beyond the cylinders, the houses
on the crest are not for mourning,
        a kind of Polynesian temple at the edge—
would they
import natives if they could,
outriggers
and various structures, to dry fish?

what they have
are two slow draggers in the distance,
    four charter boats
popping for blues, numerous gulls,
wake of a few whitecaps,
and the smoky beginnings of fog.
—the life of a fisherman?)

    "I've got this cancer;
    I get the fish for nothing."

    " . . . but he's got breasts like a woman now;
    that's not right for a man!"

    (Donna is crying)

There is a new heaviness of cloud cover coming in;
fairy lights on the draggers
blink on;
the charter boats quit and move out;
gulls rise into smoke.
Fog crosses the beach, reaches
    the base of the temple, obscuring it.
Suddenly, it is raining hard.
I see my neighbor
holding his hat brim, ducking
    among the rhubarb,
heading in. The dozer grinds into sight, and has
incredibly, an umbrella.
I think it's going to rain for a while.

For nothing, and yet
for everything in sight, Becky—
you were always happy—
only a few blocks away
from your place and Gimbels
    the clouds break into patterns of light.
Could we have talked about *light footed sparrows*

on the heavy capital at the museum?
I doubt it—

    a few gather here
under needles on pine limb: moments
against wind and rain.
I can see the heads of blackbirds,
spotty, in the drain holes
    in the cylinders on the hill.
The hawk was a large kestrel, no harrier,
but in glide,
a sparrow hawk.

—were you always happy?)

Three birds lift
from the cylinder holes,
rise up and circle,
dip, and return again↦
not redwings,
    they are grackles—
helmets of gun-metal blue
in this little light.

But the delicate drops on that river,
a spring rain,
    colors of what dampened petals?
you, under willows or old oaks,
kisses or hand holding:
we talked about that.
And a new love at 73, and even sex—
but it was not the sex—
was a clear adolescent pleasure,
at 73!

    "He is not talkative,
    not like Jack was;
        he reminds me of Jack though.

We talk very late at night sometimes;
we walked out for a soda!"

In the force of the rain, the slow
coming of fog, cloud folds
          that thicken as they move,
the houses look like tombstones on the crest,
but I mistrust it.
          At the crest, they break up horizon,
a few lights in them now;
land cuts, for their rest and prominence;
safe and happy people
inside them:
          Dream Houses, land
reformulated for them. I mistrust it—

I was wrong again—
the clouds
begin to lift and dissipate, the sun burns
the fog away, blue hat
          bobs above the rhubarb again; the dozer
has a crane. It lifts the cylinders;
grackles popping from the holes and rising
indiscriminate, in the sun.

Were you really happy?
I could ask the dozer that. It lowers
          the slowly turning cylinders
into the ground. The grackles
seem unhappy, drift
float and circle, over the fresh holes.

          " . . . but he's got breasts like a woman now;
          that's . . .

          a kind of transformation
Donna, he gets the fish for nothing.
He may be happy or sad,
          but that is our indulgence.

It is the deaths that are simple, the lives
and the dying in them
complex: we know nothing in our privacy;
it is enough
that we leave them their own.

Becky
beyond these houses of questionable taste,
now shining under a clear sky,
I give you the sea, which is tasteless,
outside such considerations, only
      it is in words this time.

But I remember
a time, you walked right down into it—
who were afraid of weather—
      in your white patent shoes,
your white nylons, your legs
yes) like cylinders—

and stood in the very edge of the surf:
the sand sucked your feet under a little,
a wash of white foam at your ankles.

You had your back to us.
On the beach, we were amazed at your boldness,
but that was our amazement.

You may have been smiling, moving
thinking of the boys at the river.
I don't know.

The fish near your feet were for nothing.
You were a beautiful sight to behold.

Standard–11,
Anything Goes (The Emerald City: A Key)

The first time we got
really close to one another, beloved,
        is when we slept together: your hand
awkwardly on my shoulder
pressing me gently for a welcome
before dropping off
at 24—
now we are 40.

Well,
at least my shoulders remain firm
tho I've sloppy posture,
and last night
walking the streets of P-Town again
a young man tried to accost me.

    hipless
    in very tight Levis & wide belt, wearing
    a bright yellow, Danskin tanktop
        (a glimpse of stocking?) & short blond hair—
    he tripped
    in an awkwardness not usually associated
    with homosexuals, turned
    to look at the pavement where it nudged him
        as if somehow the fault were there
    and not in his high shoes,
    his kinesthetic system.

    I wanted
    to reach to his shoulder & right him,
    but he was too far away.

Such a mix of energies in this strange town,
this emerald city,
        like a microcosm

in which nothing
is looked on as something shocking:
greed grows
in the hearts of enough of us
to allay judgment; maybe the wrong way into it,
but the effect's the same—

a dozen or so
obvious pupils from the local school
stand in a cluster
against the deli window
        punching and touching each other
quietly baiting
the unmixed couples who pass them;
they don't know yet
what side
their bread's buttered on—

and the women and men we might have become
(a little hip, knowledgeable, and vague)
        glance shy and sidelong
over their glasses,
in a kind
of indiscriminate longing,
        at the half-dressed
counter-jet-set children
milling in the street in front of the bakery
and the gay walkers.

Righting himself
the young man looked the other way as he passed me,
        obviously embarrassed and flustered,
having revealed, what? that he was awkward? yes,
and vulnerable—
then worked
to resume quickly enough
the grace
of his passive
stalking.

Does it sound strange
when I call you beloved? well
        what else but a little honesty to save us:
we see, daily, the ones lacking luster
wanting to touch women who will return love,
failing—
        and then, desperate—
wanting anyone who will warm them,
the turning of any key.

And I'm desirous of something
I can't put my finger on this morning,
        but there's a slight urgency
as if the water were rising
and my finger itched for the dike.

It is raining a bit,
and I suspect this early
the streets of Provincetown are half slick,
half empty—
                it's something about history
I'm desiring: my own doings last night
and ours left
only half done
in the more distant past.

After the young man and I
had done our little dance together,
I went to see *Islands in the Stream*
that Hemingway story;

you know what they say about Old Hem,
his macho sense
and his use of the word "clean"—
it's those
psychological closet critics
        somehow fearing his sentence power
wanting to denude his art

by hitting his gone life—
        I don't mean to get literary.

In *Islands*
it was the play of history that got me:
        the three sons, by the two wives,
grown into the characteristics of their mothers,
and the artist father
who loved and regretted them
at the same time
        (some typical Hemingway fish battles)
till the oldest one died
trying to be like he thought his father was,
and then the father dying
in battle, fulfilling
the son's skewed vision of his power.

What was missing was the prose of course:
that needful tension of control
        in a world where anything goes
and could come apart—
but it wasn't a bad movie.

I got out and went to the bakery,
picked out a few sweets,
        and headed for the pier to eat them
before going home.

It was very dark there,
noise and sights
of the emerald city behind me,
        some quiet lovers strolling,
and the jeweled lights of a few boats bobbing
at their moorings—

then I had this childish daydream:

The three of us are sitting in that room together
in California, 16 years ago—you
        and I, and that

thin young man
in his seduction garments. It gets late,
the Brubeck tape runs out
(he's a kind of anonymous servant) and when
        we send him to turn the reel over
he trips a little, becoming
suddenly
more than just visible,
and we laugh with him.

Beloved,
there's a power that steers these boats
I see on the bay, in the daytime
turning, often with graceless moves
        as if held in some anonymous matrix:
it's fish of course,
but that's only by implication,
                until they are pulled
streaming with seaweed and water
onto the decks, flooded with their presence—

and the town is
much more than the town's heritage,
is the young men walking
the town's streets even in a gentle rain,
        and the discovery only
about 5 years ago, that I might have turned that way
but didn't: I can see it all
as if through a dike or a keyhole
into the really conventional presence
of another place.

I don't mean
cheek against cheek or a drag dance, unhappy
gigolos, or vaseline, or some
        semi-professional groping
along some boardwalk,
under which fish in the dark feed
on the crumbs from hot dog rolls and hot nuts—

you put
your hand on my shoulder, one of the few times
we touched each other. It was never
in games, rituals, or fancy clothes
        that we passed those years together

but (tho sacrosanct) in the warm and abiding
ways of our own flesh,
Morris.

Cotton Wood

It's a lazy day—

and that means the heart beat's sluggish
    or with its stream. or more simply
just that it rained last night,
the roof held, and we've
    released that impending anxiety
against leaks and the placing of pans. and how
explain such things further?

                  2 doves sit
in short grass, and peck
above them the wind blows
too furiously for us
to get out and do things in it
and so we sit.

we read. and after a while
the pages themselves seem to relax
    under our finger tips, the light comes
again, the wind quieter now
and less heavy.

    we can see better.
we turn the lights off and begin
to think about doing things, and then

    it starts to rain again
we settle back in.

  how make a pretense of life
  as a permanence? it passes, is
  as any mood
      returns in odd cycles,

like the Cotton Wood
stood that day for us, in its menses
only in passing:
                    the bits of its aura,
some found after in our clothing—
You
were not there then.

it was somebody else I was with, you
were probably with somebody else too.
It was a lazy day.

        Look:
        now there are 5 doves.

Lazy . you read a book . I continue to sit .
get up
        go out and paint the house trim a little
It starts to rain again
It seems to continue.

I remember the way the white
bits came quite literally cotton floating
        obliquely sideways
to the road, traveling
almost horizontal to the jeep
we were in
and the green tight packed forest
of aspen .
                then
we were passing by it, one
white tree shedding
its cotton & seed.
We stopped the jeep,
        bits of cotton wood lodged
in our clothing and hair
It was somebody else I was with then.

82

the rain stops again. the doves
turn in a half-arc
        and land
in the same place again.

there are 4 now.

there were two of us—
so full
    of ourselves
we could hardly wait to get back

and made love, it seems now, so totally
even our clothes
                stirred in their places
on chair, bed and floor, came up
in that breeze
our moving bodies made
tossed out
    their seeds also
from skirt folds and cuffs
cotton wood fluffs
flooding the currents of the room

It was a lazy day.

you read a book. I continue to sit.
It rains again

    but the sun bites thru in places, enough
to send shafts of dust motes or seed drifts
in at a window,

and light
falls over your shoulder now
Here
where we both are—

for a moment
your body framed in the window seems
a construction of incredible permanence

I would call it
"this woman reading"

till I see
your eyes over my head
on the blank white wall:

you are not reading at all—
were probably with somebody else too.

It's a lazy day.

Standard–12,
You Stepped Out of a Dream (of Power)

I dreamt I saw your mother teaching a class
in which we all sat
    a little squeezed down in our seats.
She wore a hat
and under the brim her eyes burned
in and out,
her skull impossibly aflame
        under that power-mantle;
and our faces flushed
because we were ashamed,
who could not answer a single question
that she'd asked.

    And in the middle row
a woman had wet her pants, her head
hid in her arms;
        the urine flowing from her cunt
had puddled on the floor and seemed
the only sweetness in the room—
and we were drawn to her.

Although she was a spy,
she'd held the answers back,
    had changed her loyalty in our midst,
and in her effort wet herself
and I could taste
some curative
in her urine on the deck.

    The classroom was a ship—
Your mother
cracked her ruler on the wheel,
her breath went in
and came out

acid accusation on the wind
and etched our faces
with these lines
of age and ignorance.

It was a sea dream—
and the ship meandered
and the uncontrolled woman took the helm
    and forced the cutter to its course

    and forced your mother
into staggering
underneath her crown, her power
now enfeebled,
    and our laughter
now that we were cared for
ringing in her ears—
        who reeled against the railing
as the ship came in
and fled along the gangway
to the dock.

Her power-mantle lay
in the puddle of urine on the deck,
and as the ship took sail again
    our new teacher picked it up
and put it
like a tilted sailor's cap upon her head
and told us of another dream,
another sea tale
& awakening—

She
who from her endomorphic rage
woke up again, in the little lights
of altar candles
    and the cinnamon body oil,
and he who only dimly

thought that he had wakened her
      (could therefore
   place a cherry in her navel
and worry it with his tongue
in that slow way of his
while he was eating it)
could steer her into matrices
her husband had refused her;
     only the little body's exit
from her womb
as she had splayed herself
had given her
such power.

   and that he called her
"Goddess at whose feet I kneel"
annealed her
and she took him masterfully
into her own life, on her own terms.

And she was larger than he was
and huge to him,
    in translation of his mother's power
that lingered over him
       but in her flesh
became the mother he had always wanted.

  Wives are like our mothers [Fantan says].
  When we were small our mothers fed us.
  When we are grown our wives cook for us.
  If there is something good,
  they keep it in the pot until we come home.

  When we were small we slept with our mothers;
  when we are grown we sleep with our wives.
  Sometimes
  when we are grown
    we wake in the night

and call our wives
mother—

There you have
        pathology of the dream
the teacher said, its politics—

But the woman lay
enchanted in her power, that place
where mothers die,
and the childish father that he was to her
        went up in incense smoke—
her tongue between his toes,
the forceful sucking of his sex.

And that he rightly felt
there is no root but this,
        no power and care.
He sucked her nipples for their juice;
they saw things in a clearer light
and eye to eye.

I woke
and thought of Kathy and the Old Manse,
        the way the woman had used
her diamond ring to carve
the message in the window glass:
futility of name and date,
her wedding night.

I'd made a joke
        that didn't seem too funny when I woke,
that underneath the futile tracings
were the real words:
sex is life.

There was no other lesson
for me to take, except

I spend time at the sea
and if
within some sickness
        you became incontinent
I'd wipe your urine up
and I would suck the rag.

But the ship of love,
now powered by body's energy
        of such learning
in the coda of the dream
set out through fog (recessional)
to search
increasing clarity at sea.

And the Catholic, white
and summer knicker uniforms that we wore
        gave way to open classroom
as your mother's ruler
changed to a jeweled scepter on the desk
and was no longer a fearful weapon
but an instrument of charts—
        the newly hardening needle
of a human compass
that our new teacher
placed with reverence on the map.

The cutter banked
to a certain course against the sea,
        and as the ship came
momentarily broadside to the distant dock
we peered intently
from our childish comfort
at the windy rail,

and saw
the tortured, desperate woman
wave her hanky at us from the quay,

and we were waving also
as the ship turned
and she shrunk away,

and then we heard the ringing
of the school's little bells,
the peal, and falling of the leaves,

and we sang—

Goodby, Mother.
Goodby,

speck.

from Birdsongs

Sparrow

The lone sparrow comes
and settles in on the feeder
as the light fails
us and her.
                        she is pregnant,
allows us
to come close enough to see that, and when
we are almost
                        too close
she moves off: twig, to another
twig to a branch
cross space, to another tree.

her movements are economical;
she watches

us, and we too watch
as if her life mattered
        we stand there
in regard of her namesake, the small
sparrows in her;

it is no coincidence
we lack mastery.

We call it grace or the absence
of grace,
        insouciance,
fact of the mother
swollen, to her instinct to rest:
the nesting urge.

she watches.
and in the morning he rises
        complicatedly beside you
from clarity of sleep, puts
bare feet on cold floor;

who is the simpleton?

the hawk will eat her
in regard of his namesake;
her bones crack
brittle, spectacular in her death

to us
who watch her
        flammable in shadow
(which obscures her)

we are the fire.

Yellow Bird

Early morning It is so quiet
Yellow bird
lands on the feeder's rest
five feet from me.

I can hear her claws, can see
her way of movement along the rough doweling,
see the whites of her eyes.

She sees me,
hears my rough smoker's cough,
or feels some energy in
my sense of surprise
at her closeness, & then she flies off.

At once,
in the quiet of the early morning
I feel my losses in the loss of her.

   is that her
   sharp and melodic voice
   in the distance? her presence,
   wholesome, because it is out of reach?

She had
a white head. her claws
were yellow too.

She couldn't stay here.

Night-Light

The birds kick
and sing their energies in the night;
    they become a nuisance:
are they
night birds, are they somehow troubled,
what do they have to complain about
their lives?

I can't sleep, feel
maybe I'll never sleep again;
was it too much coffee, is there
something on my mind?

They squawk and sing,
they are very close
    to where I try to rest,
they are local.

I could not find them even
in this full moon.

Maybe
it is this light
that keeps us up.

A Very Hot Day

The sparrows catch the light, and look
yellow in the sun.
    One sits on a branch and turns
his breast into it.
He shines
like layered bronze as the sun hits him
and swells up a little to meet it.

You come out of the shower shining
and powdered, to defeat it.
You are not bronze
    but pounded rings of powder plate your body.
You turn your powdered breasts
back from the window.
You sing enough to keep this tribe together.

Rocks

That I had not known enough then to cure it.
had there been more time, my father
a matter of learning
        loss of innocence—
but the fat pills
like footballs, choking you.

A friend and geologist had
not known much of poetry
but had known rocks:
        "They're alive!" he said,
but he wrote poems like a virgin.

This morning
birds come I have never seen before: blue
and fat, and I grab the *Field Guide*
too late.

To lead one's life is to lead
but to follow,
as if that book in the head
flipped through
        but the birds left in the meantime.

My friend, the geologist, has since learned to write.
the rocks were alive tho
and have since changed appearance.

Turns

I want to be happy, for you
to be happy
too,
    is not always a possibility.
Daily
something discovered
that was not there yesterday,
but the mood's the same—

a single boat
moves on the bay
within my scope too far for color
    it's blocked out suddenly
    behind a bush 10 feet away—

    trees, bushes, bees
this year
indistinguishable insects
buzz in the new-cut grass.

To be happy: defined
certainly by a state of mind
    unaffected sometimes
by what is seen:
that
is certainly
    sickness, we all have—

and should we
want the world the same?

It shall not be,
is at once too glorious and too
cruel
    in its insistence: demands
us *to be happy*, gives

back the dead each year come alive
birds too various for names
17-year locusts

in our heads . And here
the bush moves and the boat's
back again, still single
turning its red sides in the breeze

while
the day turns
        and the wind turns
                my head

while flowers turn, with the sun
their cells on that side dying
their open faces
turn, against our foolish needs.

Standard–14, Bye Bye Blackbird (Toby Olshin)

Somehow,
    beautiful small bird
this morning, at the window; one
always seems to come
when he is needed: this one,
      a slice of crescent rust,
white belly and delicate
thin beak
    (nameless, without field guide)
though smaller than a towhee
he resembles, stays
only a moment (here
in the country) to give a start to this.

But first, of care and woe, the nameless
to pack it up
    in weak and sufficient
simile: a towhee
winging slowly among branches
    in the night, like a fan, those
cuts of rust—
seen, and not seen
completely, but identified;
always, it is harder
with females.

Sweet sugar of the night, night
trails in the air:
    birds the color of night,
black birds, and the creak
of gray mourning doves
sweeter than sugar.

Night's
a prologue to day, though alive:
drunks, in rage on the city's streets,

inarticulate voices
        came to me; I fancied
lost day-birds calling, an air
and an airing, through spring's open windows,
thawed, lost, and winging low,
to give a start to this—
in a city

        where I was handed
hard luck stories in shrillness,
sugar or caffeine,
the fix of your fame in public,
our name still a confusion:
            I got your letters, perverted
messages in a box. Heads
turned still when I spoke our name.

What can I give you?
permutations of Duv, Tobe and Ocean?
        Peace, of our country name?
I'll hold it for you now,
light the light, in secret?

I'll take our name
into the night, not of towhee
in shyness, but beat of the name's
echo in the mouth, "Toby"—
        to soothe even these dark birds
in the chest, trail them
from force of anxiety of lost name—
here, in the country.

But it is morning. It is not night
nor country. It's the becalmed
            waters of ocean at bayside,
the sharp glint of white sails in the sunrise,
green sea lettuce at shoreline, that
small bird at the feeder—

_forgiving light)
	and a need
for celebration beyond the name's hoard,
where he waits for me:
a confusing spring warbler (or is it a she?
cuts of rust?)
	this music the day makes
that we could dance to. You
	and I walk on the beach together;
we are thankful for no language:
yellow hulls in the sunrise, terns in the air . . .
Surely, there is some better message
I can send you?

I'm blue again, love struck
for the dead; words stick
	like a shocked wisdom tooth,
useless in the mouth
and out of it: just another
dumb simile; is the life
but a metaphor? Death is the ground
of the memory
	which _is_ the life, not spirit
but that which the hand opens to: (the memory)
tracings in palm lines,
rust cuts, that become "Toby" or any name;
only, that the brand burns in—

and that I can think of cowboys (here
at the sea?)
	and a hat you once wore.
I caught a glimpse of
you, cowgirl on the avenue,
corner of Broad & Arch (in a city)
	who didn't see me, was intent
as always, on the task at hand—
in this case hitchhiking
in a transit strike.

Your hat sat
at rakish angle, but for others; un-
selfconscious in any costume
alert, always ready (for what?) for
anything: memos, empty hassles, dancing,
I think, even
        that final activity, the loose end
of which I am left with: "Toby"
on scraps of paper
        awkward voices on a phone,
the push of memories that can't be filed
or put away with you; it calls back to me
constantly—
        Duv, Tobe, and Ocean
belongs in the country
but I'm near the changing patterns
at shoreline, and there is no
peace, here, yet.

                    (Peace—
permutations of the name come to that:
English, into Hebrew, into English:
Toby—as peacefulness.
        I picked you up, your smile was
wan, already. One

note, one
song stroke, one throat, one
bird, only, to evoke the name,
the insane desire for a perfect speech:
blackbird) here I go—

Let me forget, darling, that I go on
living; let the name be
        not a mask, but a forgiving
presence; let our face turn
waxen, then insubstantial; let
features be rust cuts on this evoking body.

To dance, to
hum to the tune while dancing, to discover,
dear memory, in this way, the late arrival,
the bed made, and the light lit.

There was light's flicker at shoreline: night
lights on the draggers; at night
        light of phosphorus;
she was white, in the moon's light
or candle flame, the light she had lit.
In day's light
sun forced upon her that blindness,
her face screwed up squinting
        in the cruelest of lights
which reflects back:
a bright skull.
                That was in a city
of variety and careful distance
and guarding,
where she carried her name in a manner
of fame, an aggressive
presence (he felt bereft of it).

But this was at the very edge of the sea;
it was night;
        there were fishermen in mackinaws, hats
reminiscent of cowboys,
poles, stuck in the sand, and standing;
it was cold (clouds covered the moon now).

And she went out from the light
in neuter garments;
        it was dark, she was passing,
and they called out to her—ignorant
and stupid—not seeing
she was a woman (their expectations):
        she had a rigged pole
and a gear box; she was passing

beyond their intelligence.
Really,
she was engaged in a kind of dancing:
steps, secret and special, that were acceptable,
because they were too subtle
for them. She passed along and behind them,
came to a place at line's end,
        at the headland, faced out
to becalmed ocean, and then she really passed.

He, then, at the promontory
in that masculine line:
no women, cold weather, and the place
lacked flavor.
        It was very much like dancing
in ego) without a partner; blues
and striped bass passing, beyond the bait.
            It was dark, there were no birds
visible, no calls.
        He thought of the made bed
behind him, the light lit,
and he pushed the crown of his hat down,
gathered the gear up, and headed back.

Toby,
the sun rises into the clouds
and the wind comes in
        (a strange morning—
it is clearer, as the light softens;
the clouds are high
and cirrus, but they contain
rain: drops already
        on the pine's new candles, some
bent in the wind.
To sing (of memory, rust) is harder now,
the day so real and the night spent.
In what way can I leave you?

104

There are birds waiting, or preening
or exchanging places in the limbs,
in the rain:
     the receding brown of females,
feathers lifted in the wind,
         rust cuts on the males.
No (rust is in memory), these cuts
are arterial red.
Somehow,
     sun breaks through in places;
the blackbirds turn into it,
and their breasts swell.

Just This

Here
in quiet of early morning
looking in
to a city back yard of no expanse
some light enters—
        its consequence
in the finely tuck-pointed mortar
of red brick, above
her window—
& then she begins to turn.

4 twisted gingkos
in this small & suddenly
lit space,
        their branches active
& their twigs some-
times touching one another
the way we do sometimes, & 4 birds
sparrows) too .

Maybe
we could put it all together, may
be the light joins us, but is
only a reflective quality.

Of the things discovered
it is she, her turns
        to get coffee ready;
not brick or light
trees or the quiet birds
begin it.

        I make
some coffee too
for you
before day starts in earnest
to confuse it.

Tools

I am planning a job of carpentry; at least
I am thinking about doing it

sitting
in the back yard, in the evening—
the light fails, and I

think about my tools
and how I have hung them up:
professional.

the hammer is oiled against rust
it is very quiet
where it hangs

in the basement, beside the other tools
which are also quiet
they

don't touch each other. Carpenters
know about such things,
or any man

who can do such things
with grace. That's why
they only say: *let's get to work.*

I
talk about my tools, go down
even into the basement
to look at them.

I am no good at carpentry.

Fishing

There is no graveyard I have found here yet
nor sought—
        middle of the narrow cape
the bay a haven now
the other side, the Sea
    its history of shipwreck.
    Nor are we
apart from that,
and in a dream last night did find himself
at edge of continent: a figure
waiting in a hallway
    shrouded, who was death,
and then was wakened to the light
from Highland Lighthouse flashing
on his wall.

I say
"himself" in order to avoid
specifics of a history,
    the graveyard I am looking for. The light
looks back upon itself; it sweeps
to inland in its turn
it crosses land
it wakes the dreamer from his dream.

America,
the nightmare in this placid zone
at edge of continent; he thinks
his dream prophetic
of his private life,
    but of your own—
    the shell of solitude
held to the ear,
only the Sea is heard, beyond
what masochistic hopes

108

are held by fishermen,
        today the bay half empty of its fish,
their nets that sieve out garbage
from the Sea.

What started here
began in shipwreck, nor could Thoreau
redeem it:
        measure the lighthouse, talk about
the quaintness of the people. There is
that mystery
of Sea that we perpetuate,
the land-locked
        quality of our lives. No one
will dispel it,
least of all the fishermen
deny that special understanding
we invest them with
in ignorance.

The Sea   The Light   The Pull
of moon is nothing
we can count on,
        think the shore still virginal;
our lives run inland
from that somehow tainted edge
of continent—

America: a house burned twice
in Bucksport, Maine, because
the fishermen disliked the architect,
the simple
        brutal power of the people here
at edge of Sea, the purest products
we believe as backbone,
rib of sand spit rising in the surf,
the very source
of moral fiber.

He celebrates himself, goes public
like successful stock,
believes the company he keeps
is bankrupt
          as the Sea is
owned not by the fish who live there
but the fishermen,
who come to dock in winter, cracking ice
from off their riggings, bundled against the cold
almost
          unrecognizable as human,
mysterious, as in his private dream.

What right to speak,
but that his grandfather fished
and took what human need he had
in bass and skillful casting of the fly,
the only real mastery
provided to his life
though lived it honestly.

     croppies, bluegill
when the bass were gone,
the scratch of scales
against his palm,
the ever widening circle
of his lazy boat—

          as in the lake in Oregon
he fishes with his brother, catching nothing
thinking, somehow
          that's because he hasn't paid his dues
as fisherman: the care it takes
the touch
the time put in in waiting,
has not learned the patience
or the rules,
          but at his current age
lays claim, specific to his history.

They come against the pilings and the dock
at edge of continent
familiar
        to their moorings, smug
as if they held the secret
of the dream he had,
are like that shrouded figure
standing on their decks. He hears
the fish
        flopping in their holds,
the lines against the rigging
in the fog.
He knows that they are harmless;
in a way, he fears them.

        I fear them.

I fear my own specific age,
my aging, gray
hairs new in my beard,
        fear the dream's source
        the loss of power
        the empty ocean below my line,
garbage.

America,
who could stand on your shore
and not say these things?
deserted
of our families
our adolescence,
        who becomes less of a child
        too soon even at 35—

Grandfather,
I want that ridiculous gesture:
        your hand rests on my shoulder;
we are fishing
it is early morning

the flies stir in motes at the shore
our boat rocks in the gentle swells
        of our movements, we are
"horsing up" our gear
you speak
in a whisper, our lines uncoil
        perfect placement
in the air.

No graveyard then from where he sits
or houses burning
        but the houses stud the hills like stone
around him;
none are open to him: guard dogs even here
and signs,
        as if a grave surrounded by a fence,
or in the hallway in the dream
the shrouded figure
beckoning
        himself to death, a final joining
of his human family;
but a nightmare
& he woke up screaming
warding off that figure
like a fish
        seems strangely magnetized
to movements of the pole, the line
invisible.

The gentle contract
that his grandfather had
        with fish he caught—
these fishermen
intent on business
        might as well use dynamite
as nets, or might as well
burn houses down
that stand against that retrogressive longing

for a past we think is perfect: America
where we have lived
        our adolescent lives out
        in a dream; this coast
this very edge of continent.
Thoreau, the beach still stretches out:
we dream we walk it in our sleep, a dream
        within a dream
within our disconnected spirits, body tossed
uprooted from our graves and lost
within a structure
        evident within the brutal business
        of the fishermen
who count the fish they catch
as money—
        coin of bondage
        coin of business
coin specific
of America, we live on
and control ourselves
        the way their boats do
        over water,
and only slowly have we learned too late
the fish have left us here, alone
within a dream
of burned-out houses and of empty nets.

It all began in shipwreck, didn't end
in Bucksport, Maine.
The house was burning and the skillful
fire they'd set, they used again
exactly as the first—

        she walked among the townsfolk
        who politely nodded as she passed
        and didn't talk behind her back,
        nothing personal in their act;

they must have seen
her house as graveyard
of their magic lives
they thought as constant as the Sea
they used
  & used the fire
as much as fish are coin
to warn their lives away
from change.

At 35
he thinks American words
to hold himself within a similar fix,
the also retrogressive
longing for his grandfather's house,
the basement
  where they tied the flies
and coated them with wax;
they seemed
eternal in their casings—

fishing
is suspension of control we need
to come to them.
  We cannot understand them,
but to break the surface with explosives
or with nets, destroys
  the entrance we achieve
or hope to, with a filament of line,
a puncture
  in the surface of their element.
It needs respect and dignity,
that elegance of posture
  sitting quietly in the bobbing boat,
  the lure a kind of ritual
offering of control to them
(the line is not a trick

but measure of respectful distance needed
    from that real world)
the nature of our contract:
a filament
    intricate, with trust—

fishing is religion
if that means
connection to the Sea again
from which we came
that brought us to this edge
of continent, and warned us
with those brutal shipwrecks
off the shore.

Inland waters
where his grandfather fished
    (when I was young) were temples,
sanctuaries
of this Sea: that they allowed him
touch of fish
    and of his grandfather's human form
(he didn't know him well at all
    was not the point)
I was a child—

but fishing
has a quality unlike fire
that touched them coolly to the bone together,
and fish
    that surely can distinguish skill
would bite the lure his grandfather offered
(not his own.

Johnny,
you would hand your pole to me
so I could feel
    that sexual tugging on the line.

I didn't know you well at all—
       the line would race across the surface
of the lake.
We touched each other
intimate at those times.
I have forgotten how to feel such things.
There are no graveyards I have found here yet,
but this is what it means to seek them.

America,
there are those of us
       who never even reached
the outer beach Thoreau was walking on,
talking of the lighthouse
and the morals New England people have.

She speaks
of Bucksport, Maine, as if
the burning of her house were revelation
of her private life:

       Divorce, when they had burned it
       for the second time: "it wasn't meant
       that we should live there."—

life with him already
going up in smoke.

She laughs, she is
       symbolic in her gesture,
       wants to walk among the friendly people,
       and the fishermen
           (her neighbors
       nod to her and smile
       profoundly, in their common guilt.

       It will not happen:

we have left it there
behind us
        at the water's edge.
And for himself
        has left it
somehow in the matrix of that lake
& gear & boat, the way
his grandfather managed
to unfold his line in air
and lay the fly
        in rushes at the shore:

it was
so irresistible
        the bass would seem
to simply come to lunch with him;
he'd merely guide them
swimming
        toward his boat.

And eating them
        their succulence
was almost
        sacramental.
He remembers how
it touched himself
specifically
        back to this continent again,
to life.

I say "we"
I say "himself"
        in order to avoid my part in this.

He sits
above the bay,

            can see
a single sailboat spar. The bay
is placid
            and the boat
as if at anchor rests
upon the surface of the Sea;

below it
            catfish, feeding on the bottom
ripping garbage with their teeth.

Between himself and boat
            a fisher-hawk
is hovering in the air
dreamlike
in his constancy;

      he sits
upon the air above
the continent and Sea

                        and then
he folds his wings together
then he dives,

pure in his anger
certain of his catch.